People of the Bible

The Bible through stories and pictures

The Good Samaritan

First Steck-Vaughn Edition 1992

Copyright © in this format Belitha Press Ltd, 1984

Text copyright © Catherine Storr 1984

Illustrations copyright © Paul Crompton 1984

Art Director: Treld Bicknell

ISBN 0-8172-1988-9

Conceived, designed and produced by Belitha Press Ltd.,
2 Beresford Terrace, London N5 2DH

Library of Congress Cataloging in Publication Data

Storr, Catherine.
  The good Samaritan.

    (People of the Bible)
    Summary: Retells the parable which defines the term
"neighbor."
    1. Good Samaritan (Parable)—Juvenile literature.
[2. Good Samaritan (Parable) 2. Parables 3. Bible
stories—N.T.] I. Crompton, P., ill. II. Title.
BT378.G6S86   1983   226′.4′09505   83-11136

    4 5 6 7 8 9   98 97 96 95 94

The Good Samaritan

Retold by Catherine Storr
Pictures by Paul Crompton

RSVP

RAINTREE
STECK-VAUGHN
PUBLISHERS
The Steck-Vaughn Company

One day the disciples asked Jesus why he taught the people in parables. Jesus said, "Many people cannot understand the mysteries of the Kingdom of Heaven as you can. But everyone likes to listen to a story, and a story helps people understand the mysteries. Then Jesus told this story.

"A man went out to sow some seed. Some of the seed fell by the wayside. The birds came and quickly ate it all up.

"Some of the seed fell on stony ground. The seeds sprouted and began to grow. But there was not enough earth to feed the roots of the new little plants, and when the sun became hot, the plants withered and died.

"Some seed fell on ground where thorns were already growing. As the seeds tried to grow, they were choked by the thorns.

"But some seeds fell on good ground. These seeds grew so well that soon there were a hundred times as many as before."

The disciples asked Jesus, "What does this story mean?"

Jesus said, "The seed is like the word of God. Some people hear the word, but the devil whispers to them not to believe it, and they listen to the devil instead of to God's word. That is like the seed that falls by the wayside.

"Other people hear the word with joy, and they believe in it for a time. Then they forget and stop believing. That is like the seed that falls on stony ground.

"Some people hear the word, but they are so busy getting rich and enjoying themselves that it cannot grow in their minds. That is like the seed that was choked by the thorns.

"But the people who remember the word of God, and who keep it in their hearts, are like the seed that fell on the good ground and grew well."

Then Jesus continued, "The man who hears the word of God and follows it is like the man who was building a house. He dug deep and laid foundations on rock. Then, there was a flood, and a stream beat hard against the house. But because the house was built on rock, the waters could not move it.

"The man who hears the word of God and does not follow it is like another man. This man did not dig deep foundations, and he built his house on the earth. When there was a flood and the stream beat against his house, it fell at once and lay in ruins."

Jesus said, "The word of God is like a candle. It must not be hidden under a bushel or a bed. It should be set in a candlestick and put where everyone can see it. Let the person with ears to hear, hear and remember the word of God."

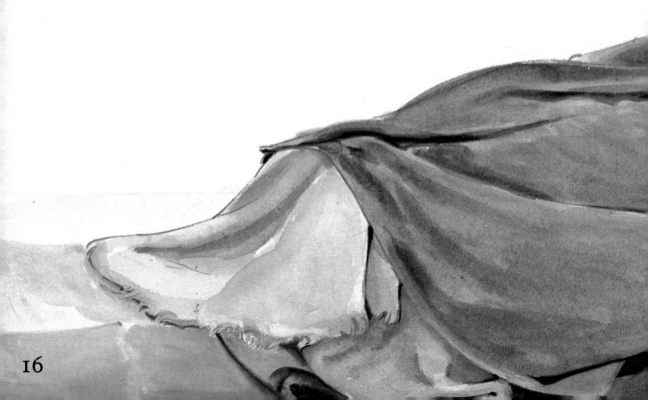

One day, a lawyer said to Jesus, "I know that I should love God with all my heart and all my soul and all my strength. And I should love my neighbor as myself. But who is my neighbor?"

Jesus said, "There was once a Jew, who was traveling from Jerusalem to Jericho. He fell among thieves, and they took his clothes and everything he had. They beat him up and left him on the road. He knew he would die if no one came to help him.

"It happened that a priest came along the road. But when he saw the wounded man, he crossed over to the other side of the road and went on.

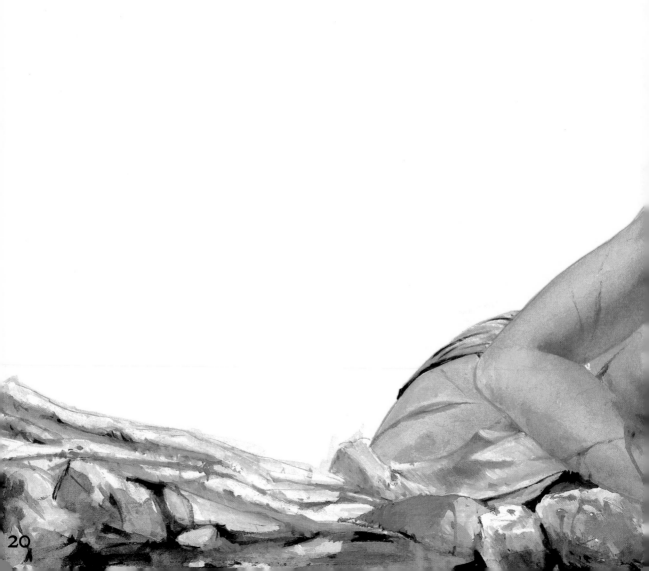

"After some time the wounded man saw a Levite, one of his own people. He thought, 'Now someone will help me.' But the Levite also passed by on the other side of the road.

"Then a Samaritan came by. The wounded man thought, 'The Samaritans don't like Jews. He won't stop. This is the end.'

"But the Samaritan was sorry for him. He bound up the man's wounds, put him on his own donkey, and took him to an inn.

"The next day, before the Samaritan left the inn, he gave some money to the landlord and said, 'Take care of this man. If you need any more money, I will pay you next time I come this way.'"

Jesus asked the lawyer, "Which of these people was a good neighbor to the poor man who fell among thieves?"

The lawyer said, "It was the Samaritan, who was sorry for him."

Jesus said, "Now you know what you have to do."

28

Jesus said to the people around him, "The Kingdom of Heaven is like a mustard seed. It is the smallest of seeds, but when it has been sown and grows up, it is the greatest among all herbs. It grows into a bush, and all the birds of the air can lodge in its branches.

"The Kingdom of Heaven is like a treasure hidden in a field. When a man knows that it is there, he is filled with joy. He sells everything that he has, and he buys that field so that the treasure may be his."

Jesus said, "Imagine a merchant who is looking for wonderful pearls. One day he finds a pearl better than any he has ever seen. He sells everything he has so that he can buy it. This is like the Kingdom of Heaven. The people who know about it will give up everything so that it may be theirs."

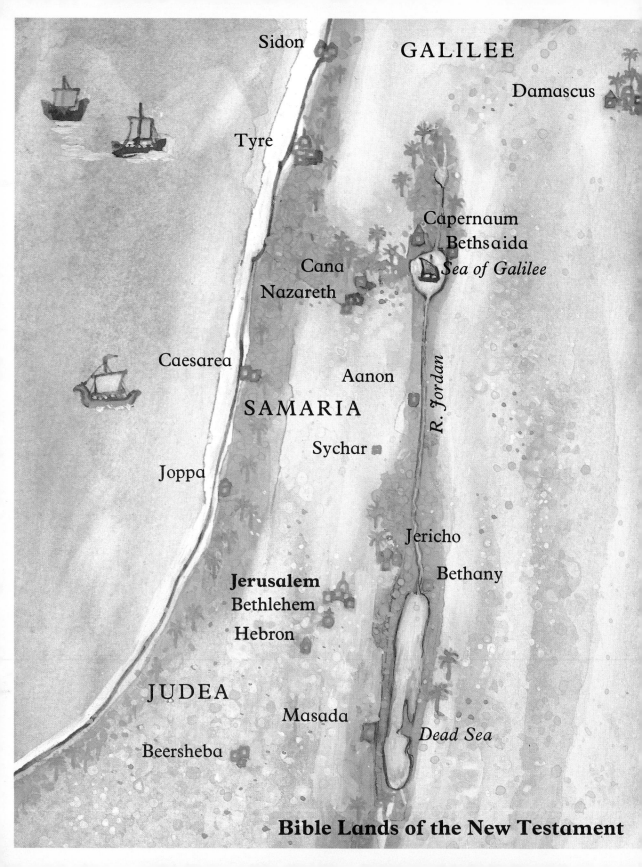

Sidon

GALILEE

Damascus

Tyre

Capernaum
Bethsaida
Sea of Galilee

Cana
Nazareth

Caesarea

Aanon

SAMARIA

R. Jordan

Sychar

Joppa

Jericho
Bethany

Jerusalem
Bethlehem

Hebron

JUDEA

Masada

Dead Sea

Beersheba

Bible Lands of the New Testament